MW00889253

THIS BOOK BELONGS TO:

Made in the USA
Monee, IL
20 April 2021

66278363R00066